Help Me Homeschool!
An Engaging 30-Day Guide to Teaching Your Child Practical Life Lessons

by Faye Badenhop

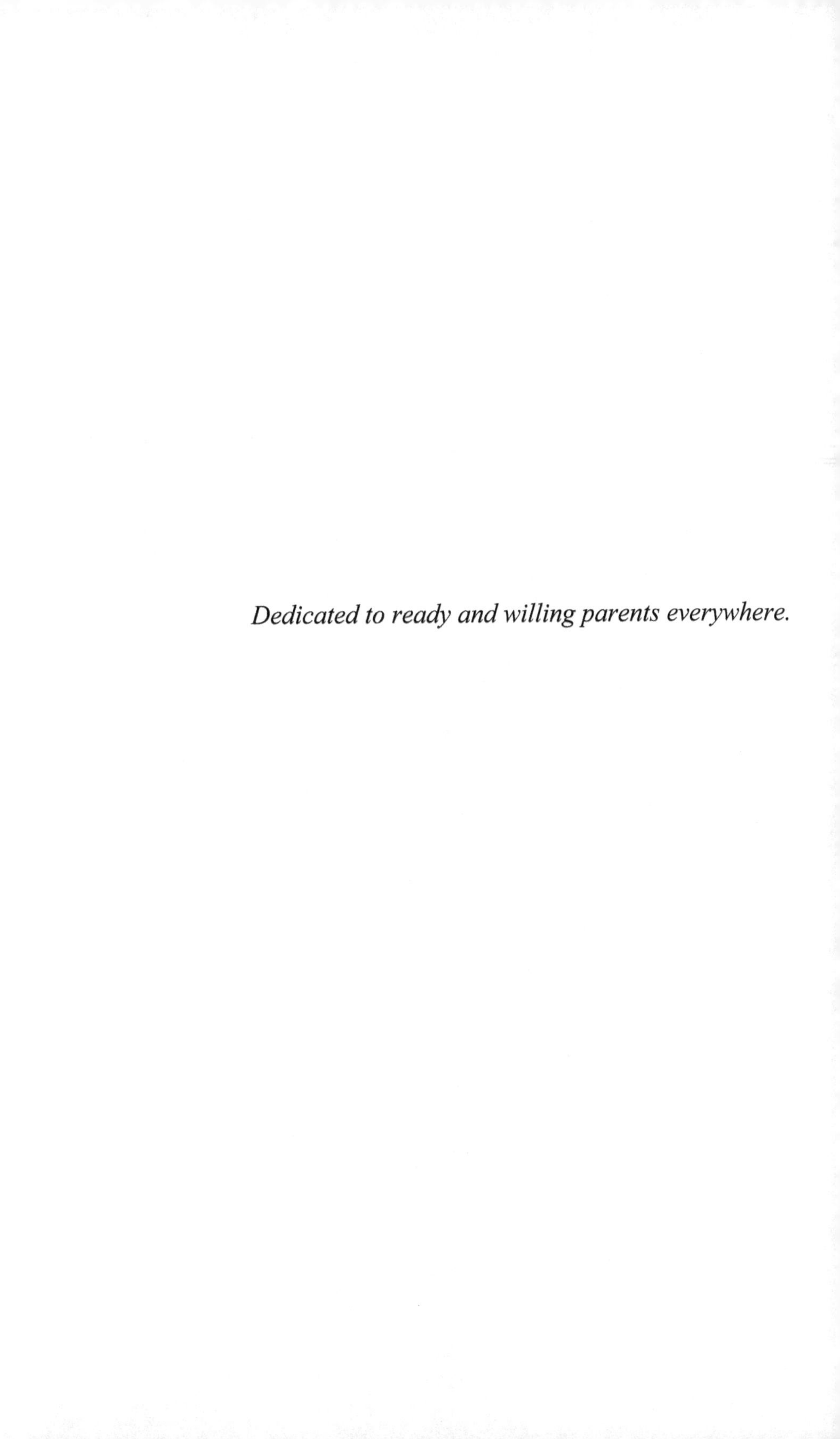

Dedicated to ready and willing parents everywhere.

Table of Contents

Introduction to Parents

Tag, you're it! Do you feel as if you were just tagged, and you didn't even want to play? Now that you are tagged, you stand there for a few moments, wondering what excuses you can use to get out of playing. When you cannot come up with any good excuses, you begin to chase your target. You think you can catch it. But suddenly your target looks too far away. You are running in circles, using all the energy you have, and not getting any closer. Just when you feel like giving up, another player distracts your target, slowing it down. You now have a spark of energy. The player continues helping as you get closer and closer to your target. You gain confidence and start to enjoy the game. You are energized and now know that you will reach your target. When you finally catch it, you pump your fist in the air. You did it! And you are so glad you played.

Did you ever think you would be homeschooling your child?

Teaching and leading children does not come easily to everyone, so it is not surprising if your answer is no. But circumstances have led you to homeschool your children and I am so excited to share with you what has worked for us.

Being with children has always been very enjoyable to me and allowed me to benefit from their infectious energy, inquisitiveness, truthfulness, and laughter. In the past, I have worked at daycare centers and preschools, owned and directed a preschool, taught Sunday school, taught and led bible school, babysat, was a kid's club advisor, was an aide as well as a volunteer at the public school, was a foster mom, and am currently a homeschool mom. Coming up with curriculum and activities comes naturally to me, but I realize that this is not the case with many people.

Now, as I am in the last year of homeschooling my daughter Mia, who is a high school senior, I am transitioning to another love, which is organizing. Combining these two gifts seems ideal to me, so I created this book to help you homeschool in the most efficient, yet enjoyable way. When children are away at school most of the day, there is little time to lead a creative and organized life with them at home. Homeschooling is a wonderful opportunity to help your children learn important lessons that they will take with them throughout life. My hope is that the ideas here will help you do that.

Tips for Using this Book

Take advantage of all the supplies, books, workbooks, and games you have purchased over the years. Instead of buying more items, you and your children have the opportunity to use what you already have. If one of the ideas in this book calls for something that you do not have at home, let your children be creative and replace it with what you do have. This will minimize some of the items in your household, which leads to better organization. Think about items that you no longer have use for, such as old makeup and lotions, buttons, fabric, ribbon, art supplies, cassette tapes, etc., and let your children be innovative with them.

Organization

Periodically, your children will be clearing clutter and organizing, so now would be a good time to gather four tubs, boxes, or laundry baskets. One will be used for items to throw away, one for items to give away, one for items to sell, and one for items to fix. Let the children label the bins now so they are ready for the organization projects.

Workstation

An important element of keeping school lessons organized and being able to work efficiently is to have a separate space to work at. On Day One your child's first project will be deciding on a work area as well as setting up a desk for books and supplies. When the area is set up, it will be time to begin the schedule in this book, beginning with personal bookwork that may come from other schooling or classes they are involved in, continuing on to the learning activities in this book. These activities will boost self-esteem, build character traits, improve organizational skills, help family relationships, and so much more.

Reading

 A booklist is included with ideas for books that can be read with the children. Some children work very rapidly and may want to choose books to read on their own when. Others struggle to get the minimum done and may enjoy listening to you read to them. These books offer a variety of ideas which work for most ages. Many of the books on the list examine the lives of those who have gone through difficult circumstances and come out thriving. Now is a good time to find the books on an online library or bookstore and order them.

Writing is another skill that we want to see our children enjoying. Do not get too concerned with how pretty the handwriting is. Some children have quite nice handwriting, but others struggle just to get their thoughts on paper. What is in their hearts and heads and comes through to pen (or keyboard) and paper is what truly counts.

Music

Music is an essential activity that sometimes gets pushed aside because of time. Your children will have the opportunity to learn and sing a song a day. Many are songs you may have learned when you were young. While some are meaningful and others more fun, I hope that singing will become an important part of your children's lives, whether they have good singing voices or not!

Art

Art is another, sometimes overlooked, activity. Combining organizing and minimizing items around the home can work together with creating art projects. Look for objects no longer useful for the original purpose and use them creatively. Hopefully, you will not buy anything new for any of these projects but will find your home even more organized and simplified after doing the projects in this book.

History

History was not my favorite subject when I was in school, but as I have homeschooled, it has become a favorite. This is a subject that, even as my daughter has grown older and able to research on her own, I have continued learning with her. Hopefully, you will be able to learn with your children also. Between streaming videos and storybooks, both fictional and non-fictional, history comes alive. There were some very important events that happened that your children may not be aware of. Each day your family will get to experience an important past event by searching for and watching a video of that event.

Money

One of the most important topics to teach our children is how to handle money wisely. Each day your children will have a simple, yet profound assignment dealing with money. These lessons will help your children be prosperous and giving rather than spending their lives working to get out of debt.

Phone Time

In order to get all these worthwhile ideas accomplished, it is important for you to have a spot for your children to put their phones. This may not be easy, but you can do it! If you must, remind them who pays for their phone. Get them on board by telling them that they are going to be learning lessons that will impress their friends and be useful throughout life. When they complete their projects for the day, reward them with their phones.

Varying Ages

Each homeschool family looks a little differently depending on how many children are in the family, as well as ages. Some parents are home and able to work through each activity with the children and some are hard at work outside the home. This booklet has been set up for all scenarios; adjust in any way that works for you. You can read to the children, or they can read on their own. Older children may read to younger children, as well as help them with their projects. Projects can be simplified for younger children, and they can be expanded upon for older children. For instance, when doing the project on Day25 where the children count their blue jeans, a younger child may count toy cars, or whatever they relate to.

Cleaning

One mistake I made when my older children were young was not encouraging them do more to keep the home clean and running smoothly. I thought jobs needed to be done perfectly and, of course, that meant running myself into the ground to get everything completed. As they got older, they were away from home more than they were home, so I didn't want to add more to their already busy schedules. Do not make that mistake and you will be doing your children (and yourself) a huge favor. It may not be the same level of cleaning as when you do it yourself, but try to accept that, and praise and thank them for doing all they are doing. Relax and remember that this is not about meeting testing goals - it's about learning important lessons that they will use throughout life. While homeschooling, take full advantage of helping your children find their gifts!

Sleep

When homeschooling, it is important to set a regularly set time for the children to be out of bed and ready in the morning. A lot of us tend to go to bed too late, which makes it hard to get up in the morning, so work together on picking out bedtimes and stick with that as well. They will be researching sleep, so hopefully, it will make more sense to them why it is important to get a good night's sleep, with no screen devices in their bedrooms. Good health has always been important to me, so your children will be doing activities that lead to well-rounded healthy living.

Exercise

Each day, your children will be prompted to do a large muscle exercise or activity. It is extremely important to keep our bodies fit and moving, and there are so many fun ways to assure we do this. This book has ideas that your children may never have tried before but may become favorites after doing them. Getting outdoors should be a priority and this booklet provides them the opportunity to do so.

Eating

Your children will be putting together their own meals. Even little ones can do things to help. Talk with them about your rules for using the stove. Show them how to cut up vegetables and determine which jobs should be done with you beside them. Cutting food up together for the whole week, as well as cooking meats, eggs, and rice ahead of time makes it very easy to put healthy meals on the table. Be creative with what you have. Your children will start the day by picking out and preparing a simple, healthy breakfast, and while they are eating together (yep, that's right), there will be a simple assignment that will get them talking each morning. For instance, the first day is, "Tell the family what you like best about the person to your right." It will be a way to start the day on a positive note, and since they will need to get along well when homeschooling, they will all need to be unselfish, giving, and loving.

Social Time

When homeschooling is discussed, there is often concern that the children are not getting enough social interaction. Homeschoolers realize that oftentimes others aren't aware of all the different activities that many of them are involved in. Some of the best books Mia and I have read together are historic, in a time where the families are quite isolated, yet they are beautiful, loving people. Whether involved in many or few social activities, homeschooling presents opportunities to look beyond ourselves and think of others in our homes, communities, and world. I like to remind my daughter that if we can get along with each other at home, we can get along with anyone. This book will give your children activities to show love and care to others. As well as caring for other people, it is important to take good care of the pets your children may have. Each day's schedule includes reminders to take care of their pets, which teaches responsibility and selfless behavior. If they do not have pets, they can use this time to research animals, check out what is available at the local shelter, or help a neighbor take care of their pets.

Things to Remember:

There is no wrong or right in homeschooling, which is part of the beauty. If you are working on an activity that does not click with your children, finish, clean up quickly and move on. If your children come across something that energizes them, go with it. If a subject takes all day, let it take all day, and just move your schedule. If a day's schedule takes a week, that is alright too. We are not learning for the testing. See? This homeschooling thing is sounding pretty good! Do not forget to take the weekends off. Children need a break. And you need one too!

Another advantage of homeschooling is that jobs around the home usually involve some sort of science which becomes part of their schooling. If there is something around your home that needs attention and is not mentioned in this book, challenge your children to take care of it. The internet makes it easy to research and figure out how to do projects, but sometimes because of time restraints we just do not get them taken care of. Now that you are homeschooling, you can be free of those unfinished projects!

If you are willing to be a homeschool parent, you are capable of being a homeschool parent. If you focus on the negative, you will see fear and failure. When you look for the positive, you will find unending possibilities. Remember that game of tag? This book is going to be that helpful tag player; the spark of energy that gives you the confidence and motivation to homeschool your children. So, get ready because…

Tag, you're it!

Tag, you're it!

Healthy and Quick Breakfast Ideas

- Eggs and Toast
- Omelets with Meat, Cheese, and Vegetables
- Bagels with Cream Cheese
- Ham and Cheese Croissant
- Bacon, Egg, and Cheese English Muffin
- Oatmeal with Berries, or Cinnamon and Raisins, or Almond Butter and Chocolate Chips
- Blueberry Muffins
- Crepes with Cream Cheese and Fruit
- Hard-Boiled Egg Pops - Stick a Carrot or Celery Sticks into Hard-Boiled Eggs
- French Toast with Berries
- Breakfast Taco - Egg, Cheese, Veggies, Salsa, and Black Beans. Top with Plain Yogurt.
- Scrambled Eggs with Ham and Cheese
- Sliced Bananas with Peanut Butter and Raisins
- Pirate Eyes - Cut a hole in the middle of a slice of bread, put it on a warm, oiled skillet and crack an egg inside the hole. Fry it up. Also, put the bread hole on the skillet to brown, and eat as your toast.
- Toast with Cream Cheese and Strawberries
- Yogurt with Fruit and Granola
- Avocado Toast
- Cereal
- Bacon and Eggs
- Waffles with Fruit
- Chocolate/Peanut Butter Smoothie (Banana, Peanut Butter, 1 T Cocoa Powder, Milk)
- Breakfast Burrito with Ham or Bacon, Veggies, and Cheese
- Toast with Peanut Butter or Almond Butter and Honey
- Toast with Butter and Jelly
- Pancakes with Maple Syrup
- Coconut Flour Pancakes with Blueberries
- Coffee Cake
- Fruit Smoothie (Frozen Strawberries, Banana, Milk or Yogurt, Ice)
- Protein Bar and Fruit
- Breakfast Sausages and Eggs

Healthy Lunch Ideas

For lunches, create simple items like Soups, Salads, Sandwiches, and Wraps.
Cook up and cut up the following items for quick, satisfying, and healthy lunches.

- Turkey
- Chicken
- Ham
- Shrimp
- Tuna
- Boiled Eggs
- Cheeses
- Quinoa
- Couscous
- Cole Slaw
- Broccoli
- Cauliflower
- Carrots
- Onions
- Peppers
- Peas
- Green Beans
- Celery
- Black Beans
- Lettuce
- Spinach
- Zucchini
- Cucumber
- Tomatoes
- Salsa
- Guacamole
- Hummus
- Olives
- Nuts
- Berries
- Fruits

Healthy Snacks

- Applesauce
- Bananas
- Cheese and Crackers
- Granola Bars
- Tortilla Chips and Salsa
- String Cheese
- Grapes
- Veggies and Dip
- Apples
- Peanut Butter Crackers
- Popcorn
- Celery with Peanut Butter or Almond Butter
- Cottage Cheese and Peaches
- Trail Mix
- Hummus and Pita Bread
- Hard-Boiled Eggs
- Tortilla Chips and Guacamole
- Apple Slices and Cheese on Toothpicks
- Black and Green Olives with Cheese Chunks
- Energy Balls - 1 cup oats, ¼ cup honey, ½ cup peanut or almond butter, ½ cup chocolate chips, ½ cup chia or flaxseed. Mix together, make into balls, and refrigerate.
- Pretzels
- Homemade Baked Fries - Cut up potatoes, put a healthy oil, like avocado oil, on a pan, spread potatoes out, sprinkle with a healthy salt, like Himalayan sea salt, and bake until crispy.
- Homemade Sweet Potato Fries - Do the same as regular fries, but sprinkle with cinnamon.
- Beef Jerky
- Almonds, Walnuts, Pecans
- Oranges
- Hot Chocolate
- Strawberries dipped in Chocolate
- Tortilla rollup with Peanut or Almond Butter, Bananas, and chocolate chips
- Yogurt
- Kiwi and Grapes Skewers

Book List

- Pompeii: Buried Alive! by Edith Kunhardt
- Ginger Pye by Eleanor Estes
- The Real Mother Goose Illustrated by Blanche Fisher Wright
- Dinosaurs Unleashed by Kyle Butt and Eric Lyons
- The Sneetches and Other Stories by Dr. Seuss
- The Giving Tree by Shel Silverstein
- Tikki Tikki Tembo retold by Arlene Mosel
- Marco Polo by Charles Parlin Graves
- The Whipping Boy by Sid Fleischman
- The Cricket in Times Square by George Selden
- Red Sails to Capri by Ann Weil
- Strawberry Girl by Lois Lenski
- Frog and Toad books by Arnold Lobel
- Cora Frear by Susan E. Goodman
- The Long Way Westward by Joan Sandin
- Riding the Pony Express by Clyde Robert Bulla
- Jake Drake, Bully Buster by Andrew Clements
- The Littles by John Peterson
- Daniel's Duck by Clyde Robert Bulla
- Keep the Lights Burning, Abbie by Peter Roop
- Emily's Runaway Imagination by Beverly Cleary
- Encyclopedia Brown by Donald J. Sobol
- McBroom's Wonderful One-Acre Farm by Sid Fleischman
- Quacking the Pair o' Ducks Case by Faye Badenhop
- Anne of Green Gables by Lucy Maud Montgomery
- Caddie Woodlawn by Carol Ryrie Brink
- A Letter to Mrs. Roosevelt by C. Coco De Young
- Sarah, Plain, and Tall by Patricia Maclachlan
- Phoebe the Spy by Judith Griffin
- The Cabin Faced West by Jean Fritz
- The Courage of Sarah Noble by Alice Dalgliesh
- The Matchlock Gun by Walter D. Edmonds
- Carry On, Mr. Bowditch by Jean Lee Latham
- Johnny Tremain by Esther Forbes
- The Witch of Blackbird Pond by Elizabeth George Speare
- The Story of Eli Whitney by Jean Lee Lathan
- Roll of Thunder, Hear My Cry by Mildred D. Taylor
- By the Great Horn Spoon by Sid Fleischman
- Freedom Train - The Story of Harriet Tubman by Dorothy Sterling

- Helen Keller by Margaret Davidson
- Old Yeller by Fred Gipson
- The Story of Thomas Alva Edison by Margaret Davidson
- Born in the Year of Courage by Emily Crofford
- Around the World in Eighty Days by Jules Verne

Day 1

1. Get ready for the day. Everyone should wash up, brush their teeth, and get dressed. Stress the importance of looking and smelling their best for those around them at home. When everyone is ready for the day, it is a good time for the children to take care of their animals' needs.

2. Look at the list of healthy breakfast options. Let the children take turns choosing a breakfast food from the list and put together the menu for this week. Do this at the beginning of each week. Work together to prepare breakfast for today. Have them set the table and sit down together. Have them drink water also. Many people do not drink the amount of water they should, so I have included a reminder to drink a glass with each meal. While eating, start with the oldest child and have each child tell your family what he/she likes best about the person to his/her right. When everyone is finished eating (let them know it's polite to wait until everyone is finished before they get up from the table), have them gather their dishes, choose a job, and work together to clean the kitchen. Include taking out the trash, if needed. I have a brother who, growing up, had to go to the bathroom *every* time we did dishes! (I don't know, maybe he still does.) Do not let them do that. Set a timer for 10 minutes and have them do what I did: get it done before the fairy comes. Who is the fairy? I don't know. What does the fairy do if you do not get done in time? I don't know that either. I just knew I didn't want to find out. Make it fun and do what you can to encourage them to get their jobs done quickly. If the dishes are washed and put away, the whole house feels better.

3. It is time to set up a workspace for each child to retreat to do any bookwork they may have. If you have desks that you are not using, start working together to clean everything off the top and out of the drawers. Retrieve the four organizing bins that the children labeled (remember, one will be used for items to throw away, one for items to give away, one for items to sell, and one for items to fix), then throw away any trash, take dishes to the sink, sharpen any pencils, and put anything you no longer use in the giveaway or sell bins. If what is left belongs in

other places in the house, take care of that now. Designate a desk for each child. If you do not have desks, look for tables, stands, doors that can be put on sawhorses or 2-drawer file cabinets, or anything else that would work for the children to study on. Put the desks in quiet areas where the children will be able to work quickly and concentrate well. Have them organize their supplies on their desks.

4. Since you have the workspaces set up, it is time for your children to do any bookwork they have to do. When finished, they may start reading a book from the book list. There is no particular order to read them.

5. It is time for music. Learn all the words to "The Star-Spangled Banner." If some of the children need more time to learn the song, write it out and hang it in a place they can look at it often.

6. Your first money project will be for each child to make a chart of wants and needs. Have them label their wants at the top of one side of a piece of paper or poster board and label their needs on the other side. In the appropriate column, they will write all the wants and needs they can think of. When finished, get together and discuss their charts. There may be some discrepancies and that is alright, but make sure each person realizes what a true need is (candy is not one.)

7. It is time to prepare for lunch. As they did with the breakfast menu, have them choose which lunch options they would like to prepare and eat this week. Encourage them to pick a variety of the foods listed and encourage everyone to try each item. If you have not had a chance to cut up vegetables, now would be a good time to show the children how to safely cut them. Remember to drink water. When lunch is finished, work together to clean the kitchen. Have each child choose a different chore each day and work on being fair.

8. Now it is time for the children to learn history. Watch a video on the Greco-Persian War. Discover who won the war and why this was important.

9. For a science lesson today, research which light bulbs are the most energy efficient. What is the meaning of voltage? Have the children search your home for bulbs that need to be changed. Figure out how to safely change those that are burnt out. Be sure to use the correct voltage bulb.

10. For their writing assignment, each child will write a note to a resident of a nursing home. The residents are often very lonely, and this is a way to have the children look beyond themselves and bring joy to others. If you do not know any residents, have them write a letter about what they enjoy doing and why. Send the notes, asking the staff to give them to people who could use encouragement.

11. Let the children choose a healthy snack and drink water.

12. Have the children go outdoors to throw and catch balls of all sizes. Then have them take a walk with their animals.

Great job on your first day of homeschooling!

Day 2

1. Have everyone get ready for the day. Then have them take care of the animals by feeding them, giving them fresh water, and cleaning any cages or pens.

2. It is time for the children to prepare breakfast. Eat together and remind them to drink water. Cut up pieces of paper, one for each person in the family, and have each child write his/her name on one, then fold it. Put all the pieces of paper into a jar. Save this jar because you will be using it periodically. Have each child draw one name out of the jar. They are to do something nice for the person whose name they drew. Clean the kitchen together and take out the trash, setting the timer for 10 minutes. Don't let the fairy come!

3. Have everyone go to their workspace to do any bookwork. When finished, have them read a book or a chapter of a book.

4. Today you will teach the children to launder their dirty clothes. Have them collect all dirty clothes from throughout the house. Show them how to divide the whites from dark clothes. Don't forget about bedsheets. Show them how to check all pockets to make sure everything is out of them. (I allowed my husband to put a load of clothes in the washer one time and when I went to put it in the dryer, I found pens, money, food wrappers, and nails in the packed load of towels and dirty work clothes! I haven't allowed him to do laundry since.) If there are stains on the clothing, show the children how to put a dab of laundry soap on the stains to soak. Let them know that they should not overstuff the machine. Have them put in the laundry soap. Have them research what is in your soap as well as any softener you have. If there are harmful chemicals in them, discuss if it would be a good idea to use different detergents and softeners. Talk about how the detergent stays on the clothing, and that the clothing then rubs on your skin. Once the washer is started, set a timer to remind them when the clothes are finished washing so they can immediately put them in the dryer or hang them. Explain that this will avoid musty smelling clothes. While waiting for the first load to be washed, get out board games and play them. When it is time to switch the clean clothes from the washer to the dryer, show them how to turn the dryer on. Then have them add another load to the washer. Set the alarm with each load, and as soon as the clothes are dry, have the children take them out and fold them to

avoid wrinkles. Have them put the clothes away immediately so they do not clutter your home. Continue having them do this all day until all clothes are fresh and clean. If there are any clothes with rips or missing buttons, teach them to repair them. Look online for ideas if you need repair tips.

5. When it is lunchtime, the children will prepare and eat lunch. Remind them to drink water. Do the dishes together.

6. Send the children outdoors to play a game of kickball. When hungry, let them choose a healthy snack. Remind the children to spend time with their animals.

Day 3

1. Have everyone get ready for the day and take care of their animals.

2. Work together to prepare and eat breakfast. Drink water. Start with the youngest child and go around the table, having them say the best thing they have ever done. When finished eating, have everyone pick a kitchen clean-up job.

3. Have the children go to their study areas to do their bookwork for the day. When finished, have them read a book or a chapter of a book from the book list.

4. Learn the words and sing "Give My Regards to Broadway." Call a neighbor and ask if the children can go outside of their window to do a song and dance rendition of the song.

5. Research the meaning of debt and the best way to avoid it. Talk about the difference between saving for an item before you buy versus going into debt by borrowing money.

6. Prepare lunch together. Try to fill the majority of your plate with vegetables. Have everyone drink water and work together to clean the kitchen. Choose a different job for each child, each day.

7. Check out the Alexander the Great Virtual Museum. Have the children tell you what Alexander was great at doing.

8. Research the ways in which vinegar is helpful and work together to do experiments with vinegar.

9. Have the children compose poems noting their feelings about being homeschooled.

10. Have the children find color books that you have at home and sharpen any crayons that you have. Let them color without worrying about staying in the lines. Encourage them to be creative!

11. Have everyone choose a healthy snack and drink water.

12. Research how much water the children should drink each day and why.

13. Find Latin dancing on YouTube and have fun giving it a try. Also, check out Zumba.

14. Have the children go outdoors for fresh air and have everyone play with their animals.

Day 4

1. Have everyone get ready for the day and take care of their animals.

2. Work together to prepare breakfast, eat and drink water. Go around the table and have the children take turns saying what makes them most excited about life. Clean the kitchen together. Set the timer if it helps them work faster.

3. It is time for the children to go to their workspaces and do any bookwork. When they are finished, have them read a book or a chapter of a book from the book list.

4. Today the children get to clean your home. Have them start by picking up anything lying around and put it in the proper place. This is a good time to use the timer for motivation. Next, have them get a bucket of soap and water ready. Have them wipe surfaces, door handles, railings, and anything else that needs to be cleaned. Have them change the water periodically. Next, they get to tackle the toilets! Show them how to clean them, and in case they are all begging to go first, let them know everyone will get their chance. Have them wipe every spot inside and out. Next, have them scrub every sink in your home. Research what chemicals are in the cleaners. If they have harmful chemicals in them, consider trying healthier cleaners in the future. Baking soda and white vinegar are two of my favorites. Now it is time for the floors. Show the children which floors get vacuumed and which get mopped. When finished, congratulate them on a job well done. Talk about how clean and fresh your home will be when you all work together and tell them how much this helps you out.

5. It is time for the children to prepare and eat a healthy lunch and drink water. Do the dishes together.

6. Have them watch a video on Pax Romana. What made this time period unique?

7. It is time for the children to go outdoors and play a basketball game. If there is not a hoop available, practice dribbling and passing a ball. Also, remind them to play with their animals.

8. Have them choose a snack and drink water.

2

Day 5

1. Everyone gets ready for the day and takes care of their animals.

2. Work together to prepare and eat a healthy breakfast and drink water. Go around the table and say something the person on your left is good at. When everyone is finished eating, have the children clean the kitchen.

3. Have everyone go to their study areas to do any bookwork for the day. When finished, read with them, or have them read or their own.

4. Have the children learn the words to the song "Take Me Out to the Ballgame" and enjoy singing it loud. Let them video chat with their grandparents and sing the song with them.

5. Opportunity cost is when something must be given up in order to gain something else. Research opportunity cost, then have each child come up with an example.

6. Work together to prepare a healthy lunch, get water to drink, and have an indoor picnic on a blanket while watching a video on the Life of Jesus. When the video is over, work together to clean the kitchen while discussing how Jesus was treated while on the earth.

7. Read the labels on your lotions and have the children research the ingredients that are in them. Are there harmful chemicals in them? If so, can they find healthy alternatives?

8. Have each child write a thank-you note to someone who has done something special for them. Have them address them and put them in the mail.

9. Let the children finger paint with any lotions that are not being used anymore by squirting the lotions into pie tins or pans. Have them neatly organize any lotions that they want to keep.

10. Have everyone choose a healthy snack and drink water.

11. Take a bike ride together. Have the children spend time with their
    animals.

Day 6

1. Have everyone get ready for the day and take care of their animals' needs.

2. Work together to prepare breakfast, eat, and drink water. Go around the table and have everyone take turns explaining why they are thankful for their parents. Have everyone clean the kitchen and check the trash.

3. It is time for the children to go to their study areas to do any bookwork. When they are finished, they may read a book or a chapter of a book from the list.

4. Learn the words to the song "Yesterday" by the Beatles. Look up facts on the Beatles. Sing the song with the entire family this evening.

5. Research what budgeting means. Have each child write out a budget for him/herself. If the children do not make money at this time, have them role play making $10 a week and have them make a budget with that amount. Next, find three jars and have them label each. One will be labeled "save," one "give," and one "spend." Whenever they receive money, encourage them to divide it into the jars.

6. Prepare a healthy lunch together, eat, and drink water. When finished, clean the kitchen together.

7. Have the children watch a video on the Life of Muhammed. What was the event that made him well known?

8. Research how to fix a running toilet, and also a clogged toilet. Show the children how to turn off the water supply valve. Have everyone look inside the toilet tank so they know how to fix it when needed.

9. Have each child make up a joke and write it down. See if they can make each other laugh while enjoying a healthy snack and water.

10. Work together to make a tic tac toe board out of fabric and ribbon. Use stones for X's and O's. Another option is to use chalk to draw a board on a sidewalk. Enjoy playing the game. Also, have them use the chalk to draw and play hopscotch, long jump challenges, and target toss. A stone can be used to toss into the drawn target. Have them draw pictures of their animals with the chalk, and then play with their animals.

Day 7

1. Have everyone get ready for the day and take care of their animals.

2. Work together to prepare breakfast. Eat and remind everyone to drink
    water. Have the children draw a name out of the jar they prepared on
    Day 2. Let them take turns naming a song title that reminds them of the
    person whose name they drew, bonus points if they sing the song!
    When finished, clean the kitchen together. Set the timer if it helps to
    complete the job more quickly.

3. Have them retreat to their study areas to do any bookwork. When
    finished, they may read a book or chapter from the book list.

4. Today is an exciting day because your children get to organize their
    clothes! You may want to work with each child separately unless they
    share bedrooms. Before beginning, make sure they clean their
    bedrooms. The rooms will get very cluttered before the job is complete,
    so it is best to start with a clean area. Be sure their beds are made
    because they will be laying clothes on them during the project. Get out
    the four labeled organizing bins. Now have the children empty their
    drawers. This is the area most people want to skip over, but it is crucial
    to take everything out of them. Have your child make a pile of items
    they do not like and will never wear. Start with one piece at a time, and
    if the piece is in good condition, have them choose whether they want
    to donate or sell it. It can be sold at a garage sale, a consignment shop,
    or online. Put it in the correct bin. Make this decision with each piece
    of clothing. Next, have them look for anything that is stained or torn
    and put them in the "throw-away" bin. If your child cannot part with a
    piece that is stained or torn, have them put a little detergent on the
    stains and let the piece sit overnight. If the piece needs to be mended,
    have them put it in the "fix-it" bin. Old t-shirts can be turned into rags,
    so have them put any t-shirts into the "fix-it" bin. Now it is time for
    them to put everything they want to keep back into the drawers. Have
    them group items together, fold them neatly, and put them in the
    drawers. Tackle the "fix-it bin" items.

5. When hungry, take a break and prepare and eat a healthy lunch, drink
    water, and do the dishes together.

3

6. Now that the drawers are organized it is time to move to the closets. As
    with the drawers, have the children take everything out of their closets
    and lay it on the beds. They will probably be surprised by how many
    pieces they own. Many times, the same pieces of clothing get worn
    over and over, with many others gathering dust in the closet. This is a
    good time to discuss the benefits of owning less, such as fewer items to
    take care of, being able to see all that we own, and more money in our
    pockets. Remind them that if they are not wearing their clothes,
    someone else may have a use for them. Have them decide which items
    they want to put in the "give-away" and "sell" bins. Have them find
    any ripped or stained items and put them into the "throw-away" bin and
    put any stained or ripped items that they want to keep into the "fix-it"
    bin. Everything that is left that they want to keep can now be color-
    coded and hung back into the closet. For fun, have them count all their
    shirts and figure out how many times a month each would be worn if
    they were worn an equal amount of days. Finally take care of the items
    in the "fix-it" bin. Congratulate each child on his/her hard work and
    accomplishment.

7. When they are finished, have them select a healthy snack, drink water,
    and go outdoors to enjoy nature, as well as play with their animals.

Day 8

1. Have everyone get ready for the day and take care of their animals.

2. Prepare and eat breakfast together. Remember to drink water. Have each child select a name out of the jar. Go around the table and have them guess the favorite food of the person whose name they selected. Work together to clean the kitchen and take out the trash.

3. Have the children go to their study areas and do any bookwork. When finished, they may read a chapter or a book from the reading list.

4. Learn the words to the song "Señor Don Gato" and sing it together. If you own a cat, have the children sing it to him/her.

5. Talk to the children about donating money to charities. Discuss the importance of helping others by giving away a portion of the money they earn. Research charities that interest the children. Find out how much money goes directly to the charity and how much goes to hidden places.

6. Work together to prepare a healthy lunch, eat, and drink water. Clean the kitchen, setting the timer for 10 minutes.

7. Watch a video on Genghis Khan's Mongol Empire. How was the empire created?

8. Research how to fix a clogged drain. Have your children make a snake by linking zip-ties together. Use the snake to pull anything out of the drain that may clog it. You may also want to teach the children how to clean your drain by pouring baking soda and white vinegar into the drain, followed by boiling water. Research what makes this works.

9. Have the children decorate notebooks to journal thoughts and write stories. Tell them to write about a lesson they learned from a mistake they made. Have them share what they wrote. Explain that sharing mistakes can be difficult but is a very selfless thing to do because it helps others avoid the same mistakes. It also helps others remember that they are not alone in making mistakes.

10. Let the children choose a healthy snack and drink water. While having

a conversation, stress the importance of looking each other in the eyes, and practice it.

11. Have the children jump on a trampoline or mini trampoline. If you do not own a trampoline, have the children go outdoors and do standing long jumps, running long jumps, and standing jumps. Also tell them to hop frontward and backward, jump as high as they can, and jump on one foot, then the other.

12. Remind them to play with their animals.

Day 9

1. Have everyone get ready for the day and take care of their animals.

2. Prepare and eat a healthy breakfast and drink water. Come up with a family handshake and after the kitchen is cleaned, practice it.

3. Have the children go to their study areas to do any bookwork. When finished, have them read a chapter or a book from the book list.

4. Learn the words to the song "Frere Jacques." Research what a round is, and sing "Frere Jacques" in a round.

5. Explain to your children which bills you pay monthly. You may want to discuss how much of your income the bills take.

6. Work together to prepare lunch. Eat, drink water, and clean the kitchen together.

7. Watch a video on the Black Death. What is another name for the Black Death?

8. Research how to check tire air pressure. Let your children check your tires and if the tires need air, let the children fill them.

9. Tell each of the children to remember a bad experience that happened to him/her. What did he/she learn from this happening? Have each child turn the experience into a story and write it in his/her journal.

10. If you have old cassette tapes, let your children use them to build objects. If you do not want them back, let them glue their creations together. If cassettes are not available, let them create objects out of CDs.

11. Discuss good hygiene and have the children trim, clean, and file their fingernails and toenails.

12. Let the children choose a snack and drink water.

13. Have the children go outdoors and move with hula hoops. If they do not have hula hoops, tell them to pretend they do and move as if they have one. Remind them to play with their animals.

Day 10

1. Have everyone get ready for the day and take care of their animals.

2. Prepare breakfast together, eat, and drink water. Have each child select a name out of the jar and say something about that person's eyes. Clean the dishes together with the timer set for 10 minutes.

3. Send the children to their study areas to do any bookwork. When finished, read a book or a chapter of a book from the book list.

4. Learn the words to the song "Shenandoah" and sing it. Have the children video chat with an older relative and sing it to them.

5. Work together to prepare and eat a healthy lunch and drink water. Afterwards, clean the kitchen and take out the trash.

6. Today your children have the opportunity to organize toys. First, bring the four organizing bins into the room that you would like the toys to be stored. Have the children collect all toys from every room in your home and bring them to this room. Work together to divide the toys by category. Any toys that are broken are probably ready to be put into the "throw-away" bin. If you really want to keep them and think they are fixable, put them in the "fix-it" bin. Toys get dirty, so have a bucket of soap and water and have the children wash them. Together, decide which toys do not get played with and put them in either the "sell" bin or "give-away" bin. If there are sets of toys with numerous pieces, put them in shoeboxes or bags. See-through, hanging shoe organizers work well for small toys also. Next, find tubs, baskets, or boxes, as similar looking as possible, to organize the toys into. It is important for the children to be able to get the toys out easily as well as put them away again. Having a neat looking area is also very important. Use boxes and containers that you have at home before buying more. Be creative with what you have. Enjoy this project and remind the children that the fewer toys they have, the less time and energy it will take to clean and take care of them. Now that each toy has a place to live, prompt the children to put them back in their place as soon as they are finished playing with them.

7. When the children get hungry, have them pick a snack and drink water. Then let them enjoy free time outdoors with their animals.

Day 11

1. Have everyone get ready for the day and take care of their animals.

2. Prepare breakfast together, eat and drink water. After eating, have the children play charades, taking turns acting out either a movie, a person, or a book. Play until everyone gets a turn. Clean the kitchen together and take the trash out.

3. Have the children go to their study areas to do any bookwork. When finished, have them read a book, or a chapter, from the book list.

4. Learn the words to the song "This Land is Your Land" and sing it. Arrange for your children to sing it outside of a window at a nursing home.

5. Explain to your children that social security numbers are numbers issued to people so that the government can keep track of how many years they work and how much money they earn over the years. Research information on social security numbers and have your children memorize their social security numbers.

6. Watch a video of the Fall of Constantinople. Why did it fall?

7. Work together to prepare and eat a healthy lunch and drink water. Have everyone clean the kitchen and take out any trash.

8. Research the different cooking oils and their smoke points. Have the children locate the cooking oils in your kitchen and place them in order from lowest to highest smoke points.

9. Have your children write a letter to you telling one thing that you do that they appreciate and one thing that they wish you would do differently. Change if you can, and if not, explain to them why you do it the way you do.

10. Have the children attempt a self-portrait. Go online for helpful hints.

11. Have them select a healthy snack and drink water.

12. Explain to the children which insurances your family purchased and why it is important to have them.

13. Find a Pilates video online and have the children try a session.

14. Have them go outdoors and play with their animals.

Day 12

1. Have the children get ready for the day and take care of their animals.

2. Work together to prepare breakfast, eat and drink water. Have each child select a name from the jar. Take turns saying one way they wish they were more like the person whose name they drew. Clean the kitchen together.

3. Have the children go to their study areas and do any bookwork. When finished, have them read a book from the book list.

4. The children may gather all dirty clothes, towels, and sheets and begin laundry. Remind them to check all pockets and to set the timer so they can keep the washer and dryer going. While they are waiting for each load to finish, get the house quickly cleaned. Have them go to each room and do a quick pick-up together. Next, have them wipe all surfaces, as well as clean the toilets and the sinks. Make a game of getting this done while the first load of laundry is washing. During the second load of laundry, have them vacuum and mop all the floors. Continue having them set the timer for each load of laundry until it is all clean, folded, and put away.

5. Have them prepare and eat a healthy lunch and drink water. Clean the kitchen and take out the trash together.

6. Bring out your board games and enjoy playing them together.

7. Let the children pick a healthy snack and drink water.

8. Have the children go outdoors and play a game of soccer. Remind them to play with their animals.

Day 13

1. Have everyone get ready for the day and take care of the animals.

2. Prepare and eat a healthy breakfast together, and drink water. Have each child draw a name from the jar. Go around the table and have them take turns guessing the favorite color of the person whose name they drew. When finished, clean the kitchen together.

3. Have your children go to their study areas and do any bookwork. When they finish, let them choose a book to read.

4. Learn the words to the song "If I Had a Hammer" and sing it together. Have the children add rhythm by hitting pie tins with spoons.

5. Explain to the children the different taxes that you pay, such as sales tax, income tax, and property tax. Talk about some of the programs that benefit us because of tax collected.

6. Work together to prepare and eat a healthy lunch and drink water. Set the timer for 10 minutes and have the children clean the kitchen before the time is up.

7. Have the children watch a video about the Renaissance period. What is the Renaissance best known for?

8. Research why car engine oil needs to be changed. Have the children help change your vehicle's oil.

9. Let the children write letters to their grandparents. Have them talk about what they have been learning. Then have them address and send them.

10. Gather tin cans. Work together to make an art supply caddy by gluing the cans together in any arrangement they choose. Decorate them if they would like. Have the children find all art supplies, making sure markers and pens are in good working order, and sharpening all pencils. If paints are dried or supplies no longer in working order, put them into the "throwaway" bin. If the supplies are in good working order but are no longer used, put them in the "give-away" bin.

Let the children organize the supplies they will be keeping into the tin can
caddy.

11. Have them choose a healthy snack and drink water while debating the
topic, "Education should focus on math and science rather than music
and art". Encourage the children to try to understand opposite
opinions.

12. If possible, take a hike in a state park or national park. If not possible,
have the children look online at pictures of a state or national park.
Send them outdoors to pretend they are in the park. Have them take
their animals on their backyard hike.

Day 14

1. Have the children get ready for the day and take care of their animals.

2. Prepare and eat a healthy breakfast together, and drink water. Let the children go around the table and say one thing they are grateful for. Clean the dishes together.

3. Have them go to their study area and do any bookwork. When they are finished, have them choose a book to read.

4. Learn the words to the song "Here Comes the Sun" and sing it. Ask your children if they would like to call friends, ask them to learn this song also, then plan a time to sing it together on a group chat.

5. Have the children choose an item they would like to save money to purchase. Next, have them make a chart showing how they will reach their goal.

6. Work together to prepare and eat lunch and drink water. Clean the kitchen together. Set the timer if it helps to get the job done faster.

7. Watch a video on the Gutenberg Printing Press. Ask the children to tell you why the printing press was important.

8. Tell the children to research what the basic hand tools are and how to use them. Let them search for them in your home and try using them.

9. Have each child write a fictional story about his/her life with no cell phones, televisions, computers, or electronic devices of any type.

10. Have the children go around the house with pencils and paper, making rubbings from different surfaces.

11. Let them choose a healthy snack and drink water.

12. Research the benefits of exercise, then have the children go outdoors and do jumping jacks, push-ups, sit-ups, and leg squats. Remind them to play with their animals.

Day 15

1. Have everyone get ready for the day and take care of their animals.

2. Prepare a healthy breakfast together, eat and drink water. Go around the table and have each child admit to a bad attitude they have that they would like to let go of. When finished, work together to clean the kitchen.

3. Tell the children to go to their study areas to do any bookwork they may have. When they are finished, they may choose a book to read.

4. Learn the words to the song "Bear Necessities." Let the children video chat with friends, singing the song together.

5. Research the risks of using credit cards. Explain how they work and how expensive it can be to use them. Look up a compound interest chart and let the children find out how much it would cost them if they had $500 on the credit card at a 15% rate while making the minimum payment.

6. Work together to prepare and eat lunch and drink water. Clean the kitchen together, setting the timer for 10 minutes.

7. Watch a video on the Protestant Reformation. Ask the children to find out what events led to the reformation.

8. Research items that can be recycled and work together to set up a recycling area in your home. Have the children label bins or boxes and encourage the family to recycle.

9. Tell each child to write a story explaining his/her life as a baby. Let each child choose if his/her story will be fact or fiction.

10. Using a large poster board, write and label the phone number to be dialed in case of emergency. Also, include the poison control number. Let the children decorate the poster and decide on a place to hang it in your home.

11. Have the children choose a healthy snack and drink water.

12. Look up and learn jump rope songs and rhymes and have the children jump rope to them. If you do not have jump ropes, use regular rope or turn old t-shirts into jump ropes.

13. Remind the children to go outdoors and play with their animals.

Day 16

1. Have everyone get ready for the day and take care of their animals.

2. Work together preparing and eating breakfast, making sure everyone drinks water. Prompt the children to go around the table and say one good thing they are going to do today. Work together to clean the kitchen and take out the trash.

3. Tell the children it is time to go to their study areas to do any bookwork. When finished, let them choose a book to read.

4. Learn the words to the song "I'm a Believer" and have the children research the band, The Monkees. Encourage them to dress up like The Monkees to sing the song.

5. Research what an emergency fund is and explain to the children why it is important to have one. Have them add another jar to the set of three labeled "save," "spend," and "give," that they already have. Label the new jar "emergency fund" and have them start to fill it, as they fill their other jars.

6. Work together to prepare and eat lunch, drink water, and clean the kitchen.

7. Watch a video on European Colonialism. Why did Europe colonize?

8. Research batteries and how they work. Have the children check flashlights, smoke alarms, remotes, toys, and anything else around your home that holds batteries. Let them replace the batteries if needed.

9. Ask each child to write down what they would wish for if they could each have three wishes. Get together and brainstorm what might happen if their wishes would come true.

10. Work together to make slime with water, dish soap, and cornstarch. Let the children enjoy the process of putting it together, as well as playing with it.

11. Have them choose a snack and drink water.

12. Watch a documentary together on the ill effects of sugar. Afterward, discuss a plan on limiting your family's sugar intake. Research healthy sugar substitutions.

13. Send the children outdoors to play tag and frisbee. Remind them to play with their animals.

Day 17

1. Have the children get ready for the day and take care of their animals.

2. Work together to prepare and eat a healthy breakfast. Remind everyone to drink water. Have the children go around the table and reveal a sad thing that makes them cry and also a happy event that makes them cry. Tell them that our tears release neurotransmitters which act as painkillers. When we cry from something sad, our tears make us feel better, and when we cry from something happy, our tears make us happier still. When finished, do the dishes together. Set the timer for 10 minutes.

3. Learn the words to "Let There Be Peace on Earth." Have your children sing and record it and if they are brave, put it online.

4. Have your children retreat to their study areas to do any bookwork. When they finish, have them choose and read a book, or a chapter, from the book list.

5. Discuss with the children the meaning of stocks. Let them know that if they own one, they own a piece of the company; if the company does well, the stockholder does well, and if the company loses money, so does the stockholder. Watch the stock market live.

6. Work together to prepare and eat lunch, drink water, and clean the kitchen.

7. Watch an American Revolution video. What signaled the start of the American Revolution?

8. Plan to bake a loaf of bread with your family. Research yeast and why it causes bread to rise. Find a recipe for homemade bread. A simple artisan loaf can be made with flour, salt, yeast, and water. Let the children know that the dough will need to rise for a few hours or overnight before they bake it, but that their patience will be worth it!

9. Have the children invent something unusual. Have them write the idea down, explaining how it will work and drawing a picture of it.

10. Tell the children to find all the grocery and shopping bags that are in your home. Once gathered, have them smooth them all out and separate them into piles, by type. Have them make a holder for the small plastic bags out of a baby wipe container, a tissue box, a coffee can with a hole cut in the lid or a 2-liter pop container with the bottom cut out. Let them be creative with figuring out a container to put other types of bags into. Work together to clean the shelf or closet where the bags are stored, then have the children neatly put their containers of bags back into that area.

11. Have the children choose a healthy snack and drink water.

12. Encourage the children to think optimistically. Play a board game together, complementing each other whenever possible. Turn negative statements into positive ones. Keep this up daily.

13. Have each child grab a pillow and try a headstand.

14. Have them go outdoors to have running races. Older children may want to run backward or on one foot. Remind everyone to play with their animals.

Day 18

1. Have everyone get ready for the day and take care of their animals.

2. Work together to prepare and eat breakfast and drink water. Have the children go around the table, mentioning one thing they would try if they were not judged for it. Discuss that we worry about what others think of us, and how this sometimes prevents us from trying things that interest us. Clean the dishes and take out the trash together.

3. Have the children go to their study areas to do any bookwork. When finished, they may choose a book to read.

4. Learn the words to the song "I've Been Working on the Railroad." Have the children call an older acquaintance and sing it to him/her.

5. Research together ways that children are able to make money. Are there ideas that interest them? If not, have them use their creativity to come up with ways to earn money that spark their interest.

6. Work together to prepare lunch, eat and drink water. Have the children clean the kitchen, with the timer set for 10 minutes.

7. Watch a video on the French Revolution. How long did the French Revolution last?

8. Research car batteries, why they are needed, and what makes them lose their charge. Find a video on jumping a battery and watch it together. Next, tell your children where your jumper cables are located in your vehicle. Together, practice the steps it takes to charge a dead battery.

9. If your children could have one thing in their lives disappear, what would it be and why? Have them write their answers in their journals.

10. Have the children glue a button design on a piece of fabric or an old t-shirt. Going online and checking out the button collection of Mrs. Warther in Dover, Ohio, should give them motivation.

11. Have the children choose a healthy snack and drink water.

12. Discuss the leading causes of distraction while driving. Determine if there are videos about texting while driving that you approve of the children watching. If so, watch them together now.

13. If you have stairs, have the children run up and down them. Have them count how many steps they go up and down. If you do not have stairs, let them climb up and down a ladder, with two family members holding it.

14. Have the children go outdoors and remind them to play with their animals.

Day 19

1. Have everyone get ready for the day and take care of their animals.

2. Work together to prepare breakfast food, eat, and drink water. Have the children go around the table, taking turns verbalizing an excuse they need to stop using. When finished, do the dishes together and take out the trash. Set the timer for 10 minutes.

3. Have your children go to their study areas and do any bookwork. When they finish, have them choose a book to read.

4. Today is laundry and cleaning day so have the children gather all dirty clothes and sheets, separating them by whites and darks, and checking the pockets. Have them start the washer, remembering to use a timer to remind them when the load is finished. Check the children's closets and drawers to make sure everything is still in order. If not, have them reorganize. Check the toy area also to make sure this area is still in order. If it needs work, have them do it now. When this is finished, go room by room together and have them quickly put each item where it belongs, setting a timer if it helps. Next, have them wipe all surfaces and then clean the toilets and sinks. After switching laundry, have them work together to vacuum and mop the floors. Remind them to continue switching the laundry, folding, and putting it away immediately when dry.

5. When it is lunchtime, prepare and eat a healthy lunch together. Drink water. Have them clean the dishes.

6. Watch a video on the American Civil War. How many battles were in the civil war?

7. Play board games, enjoying a variety of different games that you have. If there are games that no one enjoys playing, put them in the donate bin.

8. Have your children choose a healthy snack and drink water.

5

9. Have each child find three similarly sized balls (oranges or tennis balls work well) and learn to juggle. Research different hints online. I learned by starting with two balls in one hand, then gradually adding the third. Have them practice whichever way works best for them. Let them keep the balls in a place that reminds them to practice each day.

10. Research kite flying safety with the children, then allow them to go outdoors and fly a kite. Remind them to play with their animals.

Day 20

1. Have the children get ready for the day and take care of their animals.

2. Work together to prepare and eat breakfast and drink water. Have the children choose a name from the jar and guess what that person's favorite movie is. When finished, clean the dishes together, setting the timer for 10 minutes.

3. Send the children to their study areas to do any bookwork. When they are finished, have them choose a book to read.

4. Learn the words to "Do Re Mi" and sing it together. Plan to watch "The Sound of Music" this evening.

5. Find a compound interest chart or calculator and let the children experiment with it to see the importance of putting money away now for their distant future. Although it seems like a long time away for them, explain that the little bit of money they put away will not be missed, and if they start now, they will be so glad they did!

6. Have the children prepare and eat a healthy lunch, drink water, and clean the kitchen together.

7. Watch a video on the Industrial Revolution. How did the Industrial Revolution change society?

8. Plan to have a tea party this afternoon. When I was little, my mom threw me a surprise birthday party, and what I remember was making hats out of newspapers. Have the children try this today and wear them to their tea party. Look up the history of afternoon tea. Also, research manners, and make sure they use them. Have them make decorations and come up with a table setting. Help them prepare treats and brew the tea. Enjoy the tea party! Take pictures and let them post them online. Make sure they also send pictures to their grandparents, aunts, and uncles.

9. Have the children go outdoors and skip. Remind them to play with their animals.

Day 21

1. Have the children get ready for the day and take care of their animals.

2. Work together to prepare breakfast, eat, and drink water. Go around the table and have each child say what they feel is special about this moment. Do the dishes and take out the trash.

3. Have the children go to their study area and do any bookwork. When they finish, let them choose a book to read.

4. Learn the words to "Swing Low Sweet Chariot" and have the children think of a creative way to sing it.

5. Research what a debit card is and how it is different from a credit card. Discuss which card your children think is better to use and why.

6. Have them prepare and eat a healthy lunch, drink water, and clean the kitchen.

7. Watch a video on the Medical Revolution. Who started the medical revolution?

8. Gather different coins and dollar currency, and have the children figure out whose face is on each. Next research something positive about each of these people. Let the children clean their pennies in one of the following: cola, lemon juice, ketchup, tabasco sauce, or salt and vinegar. Research how these items work to clean the pennies.

9. Have each child write out a goal that he/she wishes to achieve but doesn't believe is possible. Now ask each child, one at a time, the reason he/she does not believe the goal can be achieved. With your child's answer to your question, ask a further question using the words from his/her answer. Continue until finding the true reason for what's holding him/her back from achieving the goal. This is a very enlightening activity.

10. Let your children use any old makeup that you no longer use or want. Tell them to make artistic creations with the makeup using cotton swabs, paintbrushes, or their fingers.

11. Have the children choose a healthy snack and drink water.

12. Prompt the children to go outdoors and breathe deeply while listening to nature. If possible, let them climb a tree. Remind them to play with their animals.

Day 22

1. Have everyone get ready for the day and take care of their animals.

2. Work together to prepare breakfast, eat, and drink water. Have the children go around the table and say where they would live if they could live anywhere. When finished, wash the dishes.

3. Have the children go to their study areas and do any bookwork for today. When they are finished, let them choose a book to read.

4. Learn the words to the song "God Bless the USA." Have the children make flags to wave while singing the song.

5. Research opening a savings account. Find out which fees are attached to the accounts. Many banks wave fees for students. Help the children open savings accounts of their own, either by going to the bank or opening them online. Encourage the children to add money to their "save" jars and then transfer to their bank accounts.

6. Work together to prepare a healthy lunch, eat, drink water, and clean the dishes.

7. Watch a video on the Assassination of Archduke Ferdinand II. What war started one month after Ferdinand was assassinated?

8. Have the children listen for squeaks around the house, such as on doors hinges or bed mattresses. Let them spray the squeaks (mice excluded) with WD-40 or rub petroleum jelly on the squeaky areas. Research why this works to take the squeaks away.

9. Have each child write a fictional story about what would happen if he/she were invisible.

10. Make playdough together and use cookie cutters, small toys, silverware, and rolling pins to make creative playdough figurines.

11. Let the children choose a healthy snack and drink water.

12. Help your children research how much sleep their bodies should have, why uninterrupted sleep is important, and also why it is important to sleep in a space free from screen devices.

13. Look online for an aerobics video and have the children try aerobics.

14. Have them go outdoors and play with their animals.

Day 23

1. Have everyone get ready for the day and care for their animals.

2. Work together to prepare and eat breakfast and drink water. Explain to the children how to play the staring game. Choose two children to begin. The last child to look away or smile gets to stay in the game and play with the next child, repeating until everyone has played. Have them continue practicing looking in other people's eyes when talking to them. When finished, set the timer and do the dishes together.

3. Have the children go to their study areas and do any bookwork. When they are finished, have them choose a book to read.

4. Look up the story of John Newton, the man who wrote the song "Amazing Grace." Sing the song together.

5. Tell the children to count the number of plastic cups that are in the kitchen cabinets and throughout your home. Decide together which cups are no longer used or wanted. If they are in good condition, have the children put them in the "donate" bin. If they are in bad condition, allow them to put them in the "throw-away" bin. Remind them that they now have fewer dishes to do, as well as cleaner cabinets!

6. Work together to prepare and eat lunch, drink water, and clean the dishes.

7. If you have a garbage disposal, have the children fill an ice cube tray with white vinegar and freeze. When frozen, let them take a few cubes and toss them in the disposal, running it for one minute. Explain that this is a good solution to a foul-smelling garbage disposal.

8. Have each child write a story about an unpopular child. Explain how thinking about what others are going through helps them understand other's emotions. Each child may choose if his/her story will be fact or fiction.

9. Research Leonardo Da Vinci with the children. Have them find out what his most famous paintings are. Next, get out paints and let the children create a piece of art.

10. Let them choose a healthy snack and drink water.

11. Have the children think of three things that energize them and share with each other what they are.

12. Search online how to do the waltz and polka dances. Have your children partner up and find out how much energy it takes to do them!

13. Have your children go outdoors and play with their animals.

Day 24

1. Have the children get ready for the day and care for their animals.

2. Working together, prepare and eat breakfast and drink water. Have the children practice the family handshake they came up with on Day 9, while saying, "I love this family!" Set the timer for 10 minutes and clean the kitchen.

3. Have the children go to their study areas to do any bookwork. When they are finished, have them choose a book to read.

4. Go online and find the song "Danny Boy" and have the children listen to it. Next, find the song "You Raise Me Up" and have them listen for similarities in the two songs.

5. Discuss your family's food budget. Let the children go online and pretend shop (or real shop if you would like them to) for groceries. Have them stay within the budget and try to buy healthy items.

6. Work together to prepare and eat a healthy lunch and drink water. Clean the kitchen.

7. Watch a video of the October Revolution. Who won the October Revolution?

8. Show the children how to find studs in a wall. Have them practice knocking on walls, trying to find the studs and measuring how far apart they are. If you own a stud finder, let them use it to see if they were correct.

9. Have your children write thank-you notes to nurses and doctors of your local hospital, thanking them for all they do to help patients.

10. Let the children draw outdoor scenes with colored pencils.

11. Have everyone choose a healthy snack and drink water.

12. Watch a documentary on healthy eating. There are many informative videos that give the incentive to eat healthily.

13. Have the children go outdoors to swing on swings. If you don't have swings, have them run backward and forward like they are swinging. Remind them to play with their animals.

Day 25

1. Have everyone get ready for the day and care for their animals.

2. Prepare and eat breakfast together and drink water. Have the children go around the table, having each say one good thing a friend did for him/her. Work together to clean the kitchen.

3. Have your children go to their study areas to any bookwork. When they finish, have them choose a book to read.

4. Sing and act out the "Hokey Pokey" and the "Chicken Dance."

5. Have each child count the number of blue jeans he/she owns and estimate how much money was spent on each pair. Ask if each pair gets worn or if there is a favorite pair or two that are usually worn. Let each child figure out how much money could have been saved on the pairs that do not get worn.

6. Work together to prepare and eat a healthy lunch, drink water, and clean the kitchen.

7. Watch a video on the Great Depression. Why is it important to know what led to the Great Depression?

8. Teach the children how to fix small holes in the wall. If you have any holes in walls in your home, allow the children to help fix them.

9. Have the children write in their journals about someone they would trade places with and why.

10. If there are any art kits around your home, have your children work on them. If you do not have any kits, have them be creative using art supplies.

11. Research essential oils and what they are used for. If you have any essential oils at home, let the children choose their favorite smelling oils.

12. Learn a line dance online. Let the children video chat with friends and teach the dance to them so they can do it together.

13. Let the children choose a snack and drink water. Have them go outdoors to play with their animals.

Day 26

1. Have everyone get ready for the day and care for their animals.

2. Work together to prepare a healthy breakfast, eat, and drink water. Have the children smile throughout the whole meal and during the cleanup of the kitchen.

3. Have the children go to their study areas to do any bookwork. When they are finished, allow them to choose a book to read.

4. Have the children collect all dirty clothes and bedsheets. Ask if they remember the steps to take before doing laundry. If they remember, have them begin. If they do not remember, remind them to separate the whites from the darks and check the pockets. They may then start the washer and set the timer for when the load will be finished. When the clothes are washing, have the children go from room to room together picking up any clutter. Check their closets and drawers to be sure they are staying organized. If they need work, have the children reorganize at this time. Check the toys and if they are out of order, have them reorganize that area. Next, have them wipe all surfaces and door handles, then clean the toilets and the sinks. Have them move the laundry around when the timer goes off. During the second load of laundry, have them vacuum and mop the floors. Remind them to fold and put the clothes away as soon as they are dry.

5. At lunchtime, work together to prepare and eat a healthy lunch and drink water. Clean the kitchen and take out the trash.

6. Watch a video on World War II. What were the two opposing military alliances called?

7. Play card games between loads of laundry. Old Maid, Rummy, and War are classics the children may enjoy.

8. Have the children choose a snack and drink water. Let them run around outdoors with their animals.

Day 27

1. Have the children get ready for the day and care for their animals.

2. Work together to prepare and eat breakfast and drink water. Have the children go around the table saying what their perfect day would look like. Wash dishes together.

3. Have the children go to their study areas to do any bookwork. When they are finished, let them choose a book to read.

4. Learn the words to the song "Hava Nagila," Have fun with this one!

5. Talk to the children about all the jobs that help a household to function well. Brainstorm the difference between jobs that everyone in the family should normally help with and jobs that come up periodically that take more time and energy. For instance, while washing the dishes is everyone's daily responsibility, washing the car may be a job that you are willing to pay your children to do since it takes extra time and energy. Make a list of jobs you are willing to pay your children to do and let them "apply" for them. Interview them and hire the best prospect or prospects for the job. Pay them after the job is complete, and all supplies used to accomplish the job are returned to their proper place.

6. Work together to prepare a healthy lunch, eat, drink water, and clean the kitchen.

7. Watch a video on the Cold War. What ended the Cold War?

8. Research together what baking soda is made of and what it can be used for. Have the children experiment with baking soda using some of those ideas.

9. Have the children write in their journals about a time when they wanted to say no but said yes instead. Have them explain why they didn't say no. Do they wish they would have said no? Are they glad they said yes? Why? Were any lessons learned?

10. Research online how to draw fruit. Have your children choose their favorite fruits and draw them using colored pencils.

11. Together, draw a fire escape plan for your home. Talk about where your outdoor meeting place is.

12. Download a yoga app and let your child try doing yoga.

13. Let the children choose a snack and drink water. Remind them to play with their animals.

Day 28

1. Have everyone get ready for the day and care for their animals.

2. Work together to prepare and eat breakfast and drink water. Have the children go around the table saying what they would like to be when they grow up. When finished, wash dishes together.

3. Have your children go to their study area and do any bookwork. When finished, let them choose a book to read.

4. Learn the words to the song "Zip-A-Dee-Doo-Dah" and have the children sing it while walking arm in arm down your street or driveway. Then have them go down the street again, this time whistling the tune.

5. Have the children research their favorite items online and look for the best deals. (Remind them they are just window shopping.)

6. Work together to prepare a healthy lunch, eat, and drink water. Clean the dishes.

7. Watch a video on Sputnik. Which country launched Sputnik?

8. With your children, search for information about the professions that they said they would like to pursue. Research the amount of schooling, if any, those careers take. Research what the job descriptions include for those professions.

9. Have the children write in their journals about someone they feel uncomfortable with and why. (Remind them that what is talked about at home stays at home.)

10. Have the children go outdoors and look for flowers, weeds, leaves, stems, or grass. Let them make a centerpiece for the kitchen table.

11. Let the children choose a healthy snack and drink water.

7

12. Have each child think about someone who has done wrong to them. Discuss forgiveness and how it can free us from hurts, anger, and blame. Let them know that unforgiveness holds onto hurts, anger, and blame. Explain that forgiveness can bring peace, hope, and joy, and ask if they are willing to forgive those who wronged them.

13. Have them go outdoors and play with their animals.

Day 29

1. Have the children get ready for the day and care for the animals.

2. Prepare breakfast together, eat, and drink water. Have each child choose a name from the jar and say something nice to the person whose name they drew. When finished, do dishes together.

3. Have your children go to their study areas to do bookwork. When they are finished, let them choose a book to read.

4. Watch a video on the JFK Assassination. What was the city and state JFK's motorcade was in when he was shot?

5. Today the children will organize their photos and scrapbook items. Have them begin by gathering all their photos and other items that belong in scrapbooks. Next, explain how important it is to label all pictures with names and dates. Let them know that although they think they will remember these things, as time goes on, they probably will not. Brainstorm ways to contain their memories. Decorated shoeboxes or photo boxes can keep them together, as well as photo books. Online photo books are another way to keep memories. If your children enjoy scrapbooking, there are many ideas online. They may be as creative as they like or as simple as they like in creating their scrapbooks. While labeling the pictures, have them look for blurry or bad photos, and get rid of them. If they have art pictures or school papers that they no longer want to keep (remind them that they can't keep everything), encourage them to take pictures of them first. Make sure the items that they keep have meaning to them. Do not expect perfection on this project. Mainly, it is important that everything they are keeping gets labeled with names and dates and that the memories get kept together. Have fun with this! If they do not finish this project today, have them keep everything together under their beds or in a place that will not be disturbed. Let them know that they can go back to this project in their free time. Encourage them to work on the project regularly, until finished.

6. At lunchtime, work together to prepare a healthy lunch, eat, and drink water. Set the timer for 10 minutes and do the dishes within that time.

7. When your children need a break from their scrapbook project, let them choose a snack and go outdoors to hang out with their animals.

Day 30

1. Have everyone get ready for the day and care for their animals.

2. Working together, prepare breakfast, eat, and drink water. Have each child draw a name from the jar and ask that person what they would like help with today. Set the timer for 10 minutes. Do the dishes together and take out the trash before the timer goes off.

3. Have the children go to their study areas and do any bookwork for the day. When they finish, let them choose which book they will read.

4. Learn the words to the song "Do You Want to Build a Snowman?" and have the children call anyone they can think of who can use some joy and sing it to them.

5. Have the children count the money they have collected in each of their four jars.

6. Work together to prepare and eat a healthy lunch. Drink water. Do the dishes together.

7. Watch a video on the Digital Revolution. How did the digital revolution change society?

8. Have the children work on their bikes by washing them, making sure the tires are pumped, and checking their chains. They can go online to learn how to lube the chain. Take a family bike ride.

9. Ask the children what is on their bucket lists? A bucket list is a list of inspirational goals they want to accomplish in their life. Have them write their lists in their journals.

10. Take of Virtual Tour of the Louvre. Ask each child what his/her favorite part is.

11. Have the children choose a healthy snack and drink water.

12. Check out Hip Hop and Ballroom dancing online and let the children dance.

13. Have the children go outdoors to play with their animals.

Conclusion to Students

Homeschoolers,

You did it! You accomplished so many life skills that schools often do not have the time to teach. Your friends will be so thankful for you the next time your ride gets a flat tire and you know how to change it! Hopefully, you will keep this book handy. You can repeat any of the activities at any time and if you did not perfect a skill that you tried, keep at it!

There is so much to learn and do. Keep searching and growing and loving. It's easy to sit back and take the simple way, just watching others do life. But life is full of beauty and excitement. Don't miss it!

Learning can be hard and frustrating and time consuming. But keep trying the hard stuff because the more difficult the test, the stronger you will be at the end of it! I have a sign hanging in my home that says, "I like people who smile when it's raining." Some people choose to see the best when going through the hardest times. Be one of them. Push yourself. Help anyone who needs it. Stay positive. Keep on smiling.

8

Acknowledgments

Thank you to my family for helping with this book. Blake, thanks for the cover and for using your knowledge to help get this published. Thanks, Haley, for catching that one mistake I made. Thanks to Kent for bringing food when I was writing. Thank you to Finley Kai for making the heart that splatters the cover. Thank you, Mia, for being my guinea pig all those years ago when we started homeschooling and for teaching me so much about out-of-the-box teaching. And always, thanks be to God who's got the whole world in His hands.

About the Author

Faye Badenhop is a homeschool mom, a former daycare worker, preschool teacher, preschool owner and director, Sunday school teacher, bible school teacher and leader, babysitter, public school aide, school volunteer, and foster mother. She is ready to dive into her professional organizing business when her youngest graduates this year. Married to a really good farmer and the mother of four, Faye enjoys reading, traveling to Jackson Hole to see her daughter, Haley (or flying anywhere else to be her mural painting assistant), taking her youngest to horse shows, eating donuts (healthy ones) with her son Blake, and bowing down to her other son Cory and his beautiful Instagramming wife Lindsey for giving her four of the most beautiful grandchildren. For real. Oh, and coffee, wine, friends, and healthy living. And mostly, Jesus.

Thank you for reading!